Poems the Size of Photographs

LES MURRAY, born in 1932, grew up on a dairy farm at Bunyah on the north coast of New South Wales. Since 1971 he has made literature his full-time career. Carcanet publish *The Daylight Moon* (1987), *Dog Fox Field* (1991), his essays and prose writings *The Paperbark Tree* (1992), *Translations from the Natural World* (1993), *Subhuman Redneck Poems* (1996, awarded the T.S. Eliot Prize), *Collected Poems* (1998), *Conscious and Verbal* (1999) and *Learning Human: New Selected Poems* (2001). *Fredy Neptune* appeared in 1998, when Murray also received the Queen's Gold Medal for Poetry.

Also by Les Murray from Carcanet

Selected Poems
Translations from the Natural World
Subhuman Redneck Poems
Fredy Neptune
Collected Poems
Conscious and Verbal
Learning Human: New Selected Poems

Essays
The Paperbark Tree

Editor
Fivefathers

POEMS THE SIZE OF PHOTOGRAPHS

Les Murray

CARCANET

Acknowledgements

Poems in this collection have previously appeared in *The Adelaide Review,*
The Age, The Australian, Bulletin, Carquinez Review, Courier Mail, Fairleigh Dickinson
Literary Review, Flora Poetica anthology, Granta, Island, Kenyon Review, Los Angeles Times,
London Review of Books, Meanjin, New Yorker, Paris Review, Ploughshares, PN Review,
Poetry London Review, Poetry Scotland, Quadrant, The Reader and *Times Literary Supplement*
and some have been broadcast by the ABC, the BBC and CBC. 'Barcaldine Suite' was
written for the opening of the Queensland Biennial Festival of Music, 2001 and first
performed in Barcaldine in July of that year. 'The Engineer Formerly Known as
Strangelove' was commissioned by the *Paris Review* and 'The Scores' was commissioned
by the *Women's Weekly* in connection with the centenary of Australian Federation.

First published in Great Britain in 2002 by
Carcanet Press Limited, 4th Floor, Conavon Court
12–16 Blackfriars Street, Manchester M3 5BQ

First published in Australia by Duffy and Snellgrove, Sydney

A CIP catalogue record for this book is available from the British Library
ISBN 1 85754 609 1

The publisher acknowledges financial assistance from the Arts Council of England

Printed and bound in England by SRP Ltd, Exeter

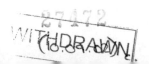

CONTENTS

To the glory of God

The New Hieroglyphics

In the World language, sometimes called
Airport Road, a thinks balloon with a gondola
under it is a symbol for *speculation*.

Thumbs down to ear and tongue:
World can be written and read, even painted
but not spoken. People use their own words.

Latin letters are in it for names, for e.g.
OK and H_2SO_4, for musical notes,
but mostly it's diagrams: skirt-figure, trousered figure

have escaped their toilet doors. *I* (that is, *saya*,
ego, *watashi wa*) am two eyes without pupils;
those aren't seen when you look out through them.

You has both pupils, *we* has one, and one blank.
Good is thumbs up, thumb and finger zipping lips
is *confidential*. *Evil* is three-cornered snake eyes.

The effort is always to make the symbols obvious:
the bolt of *electricity*, winged stethoscope of course
for *flying doctor*. Pram under fire? *Soviet film industry*.

Pictographs also shouldn't be too culture-bound:
a heart circled and crossed out surely isn't.
For *red*, betel spit lost out to ace of diamonds.

Black is the ace of spades. The king of spades
reads *Union boss*, the two is *feeble effort*.
If is the shorthand Libra sign, the scales.

Spare literal pictures render most nouns and verbs
and computers can draw them faster than Pharaoh's scribes.
A bordello prospectus is as explicit as the action,

but everywhere there's sunflower talk, i.e.
metaphor, as we've seen. A figure riding a skyhook
bearing food in one hand is the pictograph for *grace*,

two animals in a book read *Nature*, two books
inside an animal, *instinct*. Rice in bowl with chopsticks
denotes *food*. Figure 1 lying prone equals *other*.

Most emotions are mini-faces, and the speech
balloon is ubiquitous. A bull inside one is dialect
for placards inside one. Sun and moon together

inside one is *poetry*. Sun and moon over palette,
over shoes etc. are all art forms — but above
a cracked heart and champagne glass? Riddle that

and you're starting to think in World, whose grammar
is Chinese-terse and fluid. Who needs the square-
equals-diamond book, the *dictionary*, to know figures

led by strings to their genitals mean *fashion*?
just as a skirt beneath a circle means *demure*
or a similar circle shouldering two arrows is *macho*.

All peoples are at times cat in water with this language
but it does promote international bird on shoulder.
This foretaste now lays its knife and fork parallel.

On the Borders

We're driving across tableland
somewhere in the world;
it is almost bare of trees.

Upland near void of features
always moves me, but not to thought;
it lets me rest from thinking.

I feel no need to interpret it
as if it were art. Too much
of poetry is criticism now.

That hawk, clinging to
the eaves of the wind, beating
its third wing, its tail

isn't mine to sell. And here is
more like the space that needs
to exist around an image.

This cloud-roof country reminds me
of the character of people
who first encountered roses in soap.

The Annals of Sheer

Like a crack across a windscreen
this Alpine sheep track winds
around buttress cliffs of sheer
no guard rail anywhere
like cobweb round a coat
it threads a bare rock world
too steep for soil to cling,
stark as poor people's need.

High plateau pasture must be great
and coming this way to it
or from it must save days
for men to have inched across
traverses, sometime since the ice age,
and then with knock and hammer
pitching reminders over-side
wedged a pavement two sheep wide.

In the international sign-code
this would be my pictograph for
cold horror, but generations

have led their flocks down and up
this flow-pipe where any spurt
or check in deliberate walking
could bring overspill and barrelling
far down, to puffs of smash, to ruin

which these men have had
the calm skills, on re-frozen
mist footing, to prevent
since before hammers hit iron.

Ernest Hemingway and the Latest Quake

In fact the Earth never stops moving.

Northbound in our millimetric shoving
we heap rainy Papua ahead of us
with tremor and fumarole and shear
but: no life without this under-ruckus.

The armoured shell of Venus doesn't move.
She is trapped in her static of hell.
The heat of her inner weight feeds enormous
volcanoes in that gold atmosphere

which her steam oceans boil above.
Venus has never known love:
that was a European error.
Heat that would prevent us gets expressed

as continent-tiles being stressed and rifted.
These make Earth the planet for lovers.
If coral edging under icy covers
or, too evolutionary slow

for human histories to observe it, a low
coastline faulting up to be a tree-line
blur landscape in rare jolts of travel
that squash collapsing masonry with blood

then frantic thousands pay for all of us.

The Images Alone

Scarlet as the cloth draped over a sword,
white as steaming rice, blue as leschenaultia,
old curried towns, the frog in its green human skin;
a ploughman walking his furrow as if in irons, but
as at a whoop of young men running loose
in brick passages, there occurred the thought
like instant stitches all through crumpled silk:

as if he'd had to leap to catch the bullet.

A stench like hands out of the ground.
The willows had like beads in their hair, and
Peenemünde, grunted the dentist's drill, Peenemünde!
Fowls went on typing on every corn key, green
kept crowding the pinks of peach trees into the sky
but used speech balloons were tacky in the river
and waterbirds had liftoff as at a repeal of gravity.

Rooms of the Sketch-Garden

for Peter and Christine Alexander

Women made the gardens, in my world,
cottage style full-sun fanfares
netting-fenced, of tablecloth colours.

Shade is what I first tried to grow
one fence in from jealous pasture,
shade, which cattle rogueing into

or let into, could devour
and not hurt much. Shelter from glare
it rests their big eyes, and rests in them.

A graphite-toned background of air
it features red, focusses yellow.
Blue diffusing through it rings the firebell.

Shade makes colours loom and be thoughtful.
It has the afterlife atmosphere
but also the philosophic stone cool.

It is both day and night civilised,
the colour of reading, the tone
of inside, and of inside the mind.

I could call these four acres Hanlin
for the Chinese things they have nourished,
loquat, elm, mulberry, the hard pear

er ben lai. But other names would fit: Klagenfurt,
Moaner's Crossing, for the many things that die,
for worn-out farm soil, for the fruit fly.

Cloud shadows walking our pencilled roof
in summer sound like a feasting chook
or Kukukuku on about duk-duk

and this sketch garden's a retina for chance:
for floodwaters backing into the lower
parterres like lorryloads of mercury

at night, or level sepia by day,
for the twenty-three sorts of native vines
along the gully; for the heron-brought

igniting propane-blue waterlily,
for the white poplars' underworld advance
on the whole earth, out of my ignorance.

Tall Australians stand east of the house
and well north. The garden's not nationalist:
Australians burn, on winds from the west.

11

No birds that skim-drink, or bow
or flower in our spaces are owned now.
Jojo burrs make me skid my feet on lawn

being wary of long grass, like any bushman.
Begged and scavenged plants survived dry spells
best, back when I'd to garden in absentia:

Dad wouldn't grow flowers, or water ornamentals.
He mounded for the Iroquois three sisters,
corn beans and squash. And melons, and tomatoes.

Those years we'd plant our live Christmas tree
in January when it shed its brittle bells
and the drought sun bore down like dementia.

Now bloom-beds displace fox-ripped rooster plumes
in from paddocks, in our cattle-policed laager;
trampled weeds make wharves for the indigo waterhen.

Angophora Floribunda

That country seemed one great park
in which stood big bridal trees
raining nectar and white thread
as native things ate their blossom
like hills of wheaten bread
and we called them Apple trees
our homesickness being sore
if you took up land where they grew
it kept your descendants half poor ...

but farmers rarely cut them down.
They survive from the Eden of the country
because the wood's useless and rots fast
and because they're the Eden of the country.

Slashed leaves feed stock in a drought
and the tree, in its dirt-coloured bark
and snakes-and-laddery branchage
often grows aslant, heeled over
like an apple-pie schooner aground
on the shores of a North Coast pig farm.

Aged ones get cancerous
with humps of termite nest.

They shed their rotted limbs
to lie around them like junk
which only decay can burn.
A chewed-paper termite city
set alight in an Apple trunk
will rage all night and never
ignite its crucible of wood.

A veteran may drop most of itself
in one crash autumn, and re-grow from its boot.
Uselessness, sprawl and resurrection
are this apple's fruit.

At the Falls

High mountain plateau edged
with vertical basalt cliffs
like black hung chain, like sprockets
conveying a continual footage
of water, abruptly curved
and whitening down into clouds.

On a damp earth track
to other viewing points, a
young wife twists her ankle.
She falls painfully. Her husband,
his eyes everywhere like a soldier,
mutters *Get up!* in a panic voice,
Quick! There are people coming.

She struggles up, furious,
spurning his hand. A cloud
like steam rises out of the gorge.
Over years, this memory
will distil its essence: fear

of the house her eccentric man
inhabits, and what is done
there, or away from there.
That she is the human he has married.

True Yarn

A man approaches the edge
of his life, which has miscarried.

He looks down the enormous wall
of rock to the ocean-boulders
far below. They seem the teeth
in a white-green tidal blender
that won't fail him. He launches
off, just as the mightiest wave
ever recorded at Sydney gathers
lift in the chimney of the Gap like
a freight elevator, like the swelling
fore-smoke of a ballistic missile silo,
like a foam-faced cosmic air bag
that receives him, then drops back
so fast he not only can't sink
but has to cling to its narrowing
thunder-roof of drowning seagulls
and the collapse is so abundant
that, storeys above the death-studs,
he is surfed away in the wash
a mile clear of the cliffs
and left to the fast life boat.

More failure? Yet his rescue looked
like a wrathful peremptoriness.

An Australian Legend

It is the time of day
when shadows come in like animals
and shelter under their trees

when shade also tightens
in along the web of gullies
rehearsing old treelines and flood

all this drainage stops short
at a country of salt marsh
plodded in by dipping birds

this is the ancient sea shore
where the Aunt in her magic-propelled
boat carried off the younger brother

from the big island of men
to the island of left-handed women
who kill men on sight

wild mirror-image fighters
their arm doesn't cross their breasts
they strike from your own right side

it took obedience and discipline
for Younger Brother to hide prone in the boat
all day, then creep ashore at night,

lie pretending sleep and be felt
by furtive right hands, and so win
wives for his brother and himself

Bro, these people are called Women
people started to be born after that
along the coast here this happened

The Engineer Formerly Known as Strangelove

Mein Führer, they called me Doctor Strangelove
in the 1960s. This now they'd dare not do.
Right and Left then thought in Perverts, like you
but now it's Doctor Preference, Doctor Paralimbic –

I've also quit the White race. The ac-
cident of pallor became not worth the flak.
I won't join another. Race is decadent.
I lay this wreath on your unknown grave, mein Führer.

In my third sunrise century, Germany
has re-conquered Europe on her knees.
Fighter planes still pull gravities, not levities
but the flag of the West is now a gourmet tablecloth.

The Cold War is a Dämmerung long since of dead Götter
but I am still in cutting-edge high tech.
In a think-tank up to my neck
I rotate, projecting scenarios.

In one, nearly every birth's a clone
of Elvis, of Guevara, of Marilyn
and many later figures. Few new people get born
then nostalgia for nostalgia collapses.

Of your own copies, one is a Trappist, to atone;
the other went through school and never heard of you.
He helps creased, off-register people who fade as they relax.
They are tourists travelling on the cheap, by 3D fax.

Marxists will resurge by squaring sex with equality.
Every wallflower will be subject to compulsory
fulfilment by the beautiful: deprivation makes Tory.
Evolution likewise, that condones and requires

extinctions will trip the moral wires
of Green thought and become a fascist outlaw.
Darwin will be re-read in tooth and claw.
In another projection, most of life goes Virtual.

War is in space, in the trenches, in chain armour:
for peace, just doff the Tarnhelm. But some maniac
will purloin a real nuke for his psychodrama –
and not the slow old-tech sort you developed, mein Führer.

In that model, too, the screen replaces school
and language (alas, English) regains the flavourful
and becomes again inventive, once post-intellectual.
Media story-selection and, in the end, all commentary

will be outlawed as censorship. Like fashion
they will be aspects of the crime Assault.
Direct filming of our underlit dreams will replace them
and poverty, sedulously never called a fault

will be stamped out by the United World Mafia.
Generals and tycoons will be excised like tumours
if they try to impede the conversion to consumers
of all their billionfold peons and garbage-sorters.

To forestall migration, all places will be Where the Action Is.
People will wear their showers, or dress in light and shade.
Australians will learn moral courage, disease will be cured –
Here the Doctor wallowed, and his speech became obscured.

The Tin Clothes

This is the big arrival.
The zipper of your luggage
growls *valise* round three sides
and you lift out the tin clothes.

The Successive Arms

A drunk man in a rank shirt
unsteadily walks the street
begging, and arms flick up
dismissing him: Piss off!
Piss off mate. He recedes
far along, still groggily
reviewing backhand salutes
till you can trace him only
by the erupting stoic arms.

Judged Worth Evacuating

Vertical war, north of my early childhood:

in pouring high forest, men labour,
deadly furniture in hand, on mud footholds.

They eye a youth strapped between shafts
and blanched with agony, being tenderly
levered down past them by Papuans.

A hammer of impatiens flowers got him.

The Moon Man

Shadowy kangaroos moved off
as we drove into the top paddock
coming home from a wedding
under a midnightish curd sky

then his full face cleared:
Moon man, the first birth ever
who still massages his mother
and sends her light, for his having

been born fully grown.
His brilliance is in our blood.
Had Earth fully healed from that labour
no small births could have happened.

Succour

Refugees, derelicts – but why classify
people in the wreck of their terms?
These wear mixed and accidental clothing
and are seated at long tables in rows.

It's like a school, and the lesson
has moved now from papers to round
volumes of steaming food
which they seem to treat like knowledge,

re-learning it slowly, copying it
into themselves with hesitant spoons.

Predawn in Health

The stars are filtering through a tree
outside in the moon's silent era.

Reality is moving layer over layer
like crystal spheres now called laws.

The future is right behind your head;
just over all horizons is the past.

The soul sits looking at its offer.

The Antipodes of India

North Queensland, dry season 1994

Out in country like a Lincolnshire
under Divine punishment, there was swimming
with harmless crocodiles in a sheathed
lava flume, the Copperfield River,
after which antique wooden carriages
lengthened on over jade and straw plain
volcano-shot with blackened boulders.

By next afternoon, the air was layered
with heat so ashen that liquids
weren't wet on cardboard lips.
Into that evening, the train
toiled up-range towards the lights of its own
weary loco. This was point-upwards India,
back of the Wet Tropics, and almost
unpeopled. Where town lights next flared
seemed a vacated maidan of the Raj.

Robert Fergusson Night

for the commemoration at
St Andrews University, October 2000

All the Fergussons are black
I've heard said in the Outback.
Sub rosa, the Scots empire ranged wide.
I hope Scotland proportions her pride
now to the faith her lads kept with
all the subject folks they slept with.
I know for you this wasn't an issue.
Madness made a white man of you

disastrously young. You stayed alive
just long enough to revive
from Scottish models and kings
such mediaeval things
as documentary verse-television
and writing in Scots for the brain.
In that, you set the great precedent
for every vernacular and variant

the world-reach of English would present.
Now you're two hundred and fifty
and gin some power the giftie
gied ye of a writership-in-revenance

you'd find a death-cult called Romance
both selling and preserving a scrubbed Reekie
and the now-posh Highlands. Very freaky.
You might outdo Dr Johnson in polite

St Andrews now, that Reformation bombsite.
I fear you mightn't outdraw golf there:
golf keeps from the door the wolf there –
but no one does what you showed some aversion
to already in your time, poetical inversion.
Metrics too, now, are Triassic pent amateur
and 'Rhyme is for Negroes', I heard in Berlin:
the speaker was a literary Finn.

Such talk, now at last, is a sin
in place of much that wasn't. Madness
for instance. The Bedlams yielded to medicine:
even madness has, a little. Madness:
would you rise from the grave back through madness?
It took you and left us Burns
of the Night. Many jubilant returns:
this at last is Robert Fergusson Night.

To Dye For

A razor whetting silt and alluvium
off a neck in a mirror-doubled room
of soak and frizz and conversation
piling curlers and the hush-hush spray
and with the wide canny old shop broom
the work-experience schoolgirl hourly
angles and felts together
the one uncontentious human flag,
grey ginger lilac buff
black blonde and coherent brown.

Touchdown

The great airliner has been filled
all night with a huge sibilance
which would rhyme with FORTH
but now it banks, lets sunrise
in in freak lemon Kliegs,
eases down like a brushstroke
onto swift cement, and throws out
its hurricane of air anchors.
Soon we'll all be standing
encumbered and forbidding in the aisles
till the heads of those farthest forward
start rocking side to side, leaving,
and that will spread back:
we'll all start swaying along as
people do on planks but not on streets,
our heads tick-tocking with times
that are wrong everywhere.

than half an hour plus time added on to wrest the ball back from Talorca and score. If they didn't act decisively, their first ever chance of winning a trophy would be going straight down the drain.

The Cut-Out

In the shed it's bumped verticals,
tin and planking the colour of rain.

The sheep left their cloud inside
and two men lie wringing wet.

One man owns the flock, but neither
expects to wear the suitings.

The indoor storm of their work
earns a bit more survival, near home,

and each shearing-sling is a whale's
joined jawbones, dangling from a spring.

History of the Enlightenment

Faith was a dream technology
but one we couldn't master, or do cold
and it soon became equivocal again.
Mountains got moved by money or the lash
and we started to insult faith
as if it might be piqued and after all
kick in that sacred phase-shift
where cancers vanish, and the
golden brown in their antique clothes
enlarge from photograph size, walking
toward us, all welcoming, with secrets
the day it is Dreamtime in our streets.

Visitor

He knocks at the door
and listens to his heart approaching.

Mythology

A stupefying peak crack
across boiling air miles,
instantaneously annulled. That
was one of the Lightning brothers.
Brilliant longer than their lifetimes
they exist in orgasm only.
Between, they're air's memory
of climax. Death rays hid in hum.
Who'll fish the blind scrawl of lightning
out of Life's mouth, that old clay golem?
Eye-jabbing forerunners of live wire
their yield's that mirror perfume
mounting up to tame the Sun.

Clothing as Dwelling as Shouldered Boat

Propped sheets of bark converging
over skin-oils and a winter fire,
stitched hides of a furry rug-cloak
with their naked backs to the weather,
clothing as dwelling as shouldered boat
beetle-backed, with bending ridgelines,
all this, resurrected and gigantic:
the Opera House,
Sydney's Aboriginal building.

Starry Night

In the late Nineteenth century
one is out painting landscapes
with spiralling sky
and helicopter lights approaching.

The Kettle's Bubble-Making Floor

Who remembers the bitter
smell of smoke still in the house
the sunny next afternoon?
So recently smoke was everyday.
Who remembers the woolly
pink inside a burning peat?
The taste of tank water boiled
in blanched, black-shelled cast iron?
The pucker of water heated with
ashy stones in a wooden dish?

Big Bang

If everything is receding
from everything, we're only
seeing the backs of the stars.

Worker Knowledge

The very slight S of an adze handle
or broadaxe handle are cut off square.
When adzes stopped licking timber ships
they were stubbed to scrape rabbit-trap setts.

But the worker's end of a felling axe
where the tapering upsweep levels down
to bulge, is cut slant, to the shape
of a thoroughbred's hoof pawing the ground.

41

Jellyfish

Globe globe globe globe
soft glass bowls upside down
over serves of nutty udder and teats
under the surface of the sun.

To Fly In Just Your Suit

Humans are flown, or fall;
humans can't fly.
We're down with the gravity-lumpers,
rare, thick-boned, often basso.

Most animals above the tides are airborne.
Typically tuned keen, they
throw the ground away with wire feet
and swoop rings round it.

Magpies, listening askance
for their food in and under lawn,
strut so hairtrigger they almost
dangle on earth, out of the air.

Nearly anything can make their
tailcoats break into wings.

The Great Cuisine Cleaver Dance Sonnet

Juice-wet black steel
rectangle with square bite
dock pork slice slice
candy pork mouth size
heel-and-toe work walk
thru greens wad widths
bloc duck bisect bone
facet glaze nick snake
slit wriggle take gallbladder
whop garlic shave lily-root
wham! clay chicken-crust
hiss wok plug flare
circling soy cringing prawn
blade amassing sideways mince.

Lace Curtain

All politeness, all endearments
are known as palaver
once you are inside that love.
It is a compound
to keep out the world, and nearly everyone
even within it has a contempt-name.
You are in on a stare,
a style of looking down,
and what is counted worth saying
is what has turned all stuff
that housefly colour.

Creole Exam

How old were you when you first
lived in a weatherproof house?

The Hewers

He used the older Irish profanity:
the hammer wriggled its bottom,
the heavens wore skimpy garish clothes,
the science of physics cruised men
who ogled it out of slow cars –
he put no limit to the fabulous
variety of entities
that might offer sex for money.

Laggan Cemetery

Sheep are like legal wigs
the colour of fissured cement
in that bleached country
and the few one-storey buildings
of the living can't dwarf the
absorbed marble chess of the dead.

The Paint House

That house on the riverbank
below the high guillotine bridge
was of planking, but no light came out
through the joins. It didn't draw.
It turned a back on us like cheering
heard differently from year to year.

Gloss black on gut-pink with chartreuse
patched over both, all ignoring its house-shapes:
some said whatever remained in paint tins
was the design principle. Decades before hippiedom.
Next year it might be lime and navy blue
invading the cherry roof to big extents.
It was my first half dozen abstract paintings.

I hear the man who owned it was a Bird.

Hoon Hoon

Hoon, hoon, that blowfly croon:
first a pimp and then a goon.
Sound of a prop plane crossing the moon.
The crack of noon from a can of beer
and a Viking is nothing but a rune hoon.

A Countryman

On the long flats north of the river
an elder in a leather jacket
is hitchhiking to his daughter's funeral.

The End of Symbol

From a cinder in the far blue
a wedgetail eagle used to magnify
down into arrival, into belief,
matching speeds with a boy as he
rode his bike through suburban Melbourne,
then it would fold double and alight
on his handlebars, its inarguable expression
never ruffled, but its flickknife pinions
dilating around curves, and it would
chicken-peep near inaudibly when he
caressed it beneath the flames of its neck.

The Scores

Australia since Federation

1901

When we were all servants
scrubbing off Madam's slurs
I gave up my baby
and the black girl kept hers.
When I got my own high horse
living things felt my spurs
and the flowers were all golden wattle.

1921

That weak word the *Battlers*:
I saw from the train
families punch hoods from wheat bags
to keep out the rain;
Tom said a seller's market
made Australian girls vain
and for Tom the flowers were poppies.

1941

Ar there, Ginger Meggs:
was it Susso tea and suet
put those calipers on your legs?
If Sister Kenny could do it

53

you'd walk again like a trooper,
left-right and left-right
and the wreaths would be Singapore orchids.

1961
We came because here were no politics
said your in-laws. *Sweet monotonous languor!*
and a *pill* was a sexless bore at school
but one brought bassinettes under control;
you were young and free for longer:
somehow this caused great anger
and soon flowers came by wire from America.

1981
You rose climbing up,
you rose going down
as snide peace with few imports
hung on in your home town.
When green learned to rust iron
dinners dared not be brown
and the flowers were flung gladioli.

2001
Fashion ruled, but another queen reigned.
Some flickers of nonsense remained:
It's evening here, Nonna, so hey!
The world won't be ending today.

One last war-trip, and none of ours killed!
Collective rights alone were instilled;
the singular was gagged and at bay
and the flowers were Olympic Gold roses.

Reclaim the Sites

We are spared the Avenues of Liberation
and the water-cannoned Fifths of May
but I tire of cities clogged with salutes
to other cities: York, Liverpool, Oxford Streets
and memorial royalty: Elizabeth,
Albert, William, unnumbered George.
Give me Sallie Huckstepp Road, ahead of
sepia Sussex, or Argyle, or Yankee numbering
– and why not a whole metropolis
street-signed for its own life and ours:
Childsplay Park and First Bra Avenue,
Unsecured Loan, the Boulevard Kiss,
Radar Strip, Bread-Fragrance Corner,
Fumbletrouser, Delight Bridge, Timeless Square?

The Clear Saline of Theory

Theory has done this:
orphans are filing into school
in the tropical 1940s
and every one of them has parents
living, who try to write to them.
Successive tides of theory
flood the poorest faces with salt.

The Fair Go

A ginger-biscuit kelpie dog,
young, abandoned off the highway
up a gravel road. Livestock
and rifle country, so the big
harp of ribs in its mouth
as its start in life is
butcher-cut. To prove innocence.

The Bellwether Brush

As the painter Sali Herman discerns
and captures the iron-lace character
of what are still called slums then
he's unaware the bright haze his brush
confers is called Billions;
he delightedly thinks Beauty, Truth,
but fashion turns its head, and starts
walking clap-clap in the footsteps,
clap-clap, of his easel,
walking in twos, as coppers used to,
till the salt of the earth accept
hot offers for their bijou homes.

In a Time of Cuisine

A fact the gourmet
euphemism can't silence:
vegetarians eat sex,
carnivores eat violence.

Uplands

Across silvering cobble
                    into white-ant stump country.

Hills lie where they fell;
                    boulders sultana their steeps.

Smoke wanders up from a couple of far places.

Crested trees pour their shade
                    to one side on the ground.

Unplugging their weight,
                    kangaroos hoist up, and bounce.

A hill's front becoming its back
                    takes the sun all day.

Forest up some slopes,
                    thin enough to see grass under.

Getting well out now
                    back into the high country.

Mountains pregnant with hills in a white skim sky.

The Pay for Fosterage

The carpenter could have stayed
hunched over, at work on his chagrin,
left everything to the hush-ups
and stone-evadings of women.
He could have escaped the thousands
of years of speculation. The horns.
But all that weakness was behind him.
The courteous presence had spoken
unearthly sense to its equal,
himself. As he would be from now
on into the world to come.

The Myriads

Resolute, you come to a cell
and its powers are all wrong.
It can never make your great tree
with you. And it was your chance.

Pine pollen on the water
making sallow jade islands
in the evening sun.

A Study of the Nude

Someone naked with you
will rarely be a nude.
A nude is never with just one.

Nude looks back at everyone
or no one. Aubergine or bluish rose,
a nude is a generalization.

Someone has given their name
and face to be face all over,
to be the face of something

that isn't for caressing
except with the mind's hand.
Nude is the full dress of undressing.

Iguassu

Shallow at brinks
with pouring tussocks
a bolt of live tan water
is continuously tugged
off miles of table
by thunderous white claws.

Pietà Once Attributed to Cosme Tura

This is the nadir of the story.

His mother's hairpiece, her *sheitel*,
is torn away, her own cropped hair looks burnt.
She had said the first Mass
and made Godhead a fact
which his strangeness had kept proving,
but what of that is still true
now, with his limp weight at her knee?
Her arms open, and withdraw,
and come back. That first eucharist
she could have been stoned to death for
is still alive in her body.

The Knockdown Question

Why does God not spare the innocent?

The answer to that is not in
the same world as the question
so you would shrink from me
in terror if I could answer it.

The Insiders

What's in who for you?
Who's in you for himself?

The Onset

Rain. Its breath a liquid dust
ages the brooding European
overcoat movie in the pond,
then it prickles, across the deep
windows there, then blinks
with excited eyelids, pinging
all rings like the dimples
on a steel-band drum, and soon
the closed velvet doors
of the still theatre have vanished
under shoal like tin lids dancing
massed pinches of potato water.

The Dog's Bad Name

My politics are like crop circles
that appear in angry wheat.

The sourest explanations of them
get force-fed to undefended minds.

I never know their outlines in advance;
all I know is, no group makes them.

What strikes me more is the frequent
wealth of the estates they afflict.

Pop Music

Empty as a country town street
after five. Two or three crisp
high-heel walkers, and a pair
of little girls in a station wagon,
one bunging a pop bottle *boinc*
against her head and *bocc*
against the wagon. The other blows
music into hers: *Doe roe to hoe soon*
but no throe for woe yet, moon!

The Body in Physics

The air has sides, in a house.
Birds, whacked from colliding, embrace
its sheer with umbrella-rib skiddings.
They gape silent death-cries when closed
in converging hands, or snatched out
of such parts of their theory as still fly.
Carried outside, they pause a beat
and drop upwards, into gravity that once more
blows as well as sucks. Fliers' gravity.

Fruit Bat Colony by Day

High above its gloom
this forest is all hung
with head-down ginger bats
like big leather bees.

In sun to stay drowsy
daylong in slow dangle
chi-chi as monkeys
they blow on sad tin horns,
glide, nurture babies, sleep,
waiting for their real lives.

Cool History

Identity oversimplifies humans.
It denies the hybrid, as trees can't.

Trees, which wrap height in pages
self-knitted from ground water and light

are stood scrolls best read unopened.
They lean to each other and away

in politics of sun-rivalry
or at knotted behests in the earth.

Billets cut from them are tight-bound
photocopies detailing food and ancestry.

Eons on, their concentric years
will be eloquent on suffering and old airs.

The Machine-Gunning of Charm

Happy the city that stayed poorish
or unbombed through the twentieth century
and never rebuilt itself then.

All centuries back to the tenth
in the West, could put up more humane
ordinary and pretty-good buildings:

undercrofts, fat colonnades, gingerbread,
crooked corridors with much later privy,
street fronts bluff as God Save the King.

The twentieth century grew such icy
ambition and scorn that it built marvels
or else crap. Over charm's mass grave

its middle range gridded medicine's extra
billions in a punitive mediocrity.

The Climax of Factory Farming

Farm gates were sealed with tape;
people couldn't stop shaking their heads.
Out on the fells and low fields
in twilight, it was the Satanic mills
come again: the farm beasts of Britain
being burnt inside walls of their feed.

Massacre's All-Party Fuel

The cones of the Wollemi pine
erupt at the ends of its branches
like the stars of the Eureka flag.
I grew up in the early country
and Libra put her sword up my nose
and taught me her values: *on the*
other hand, but then on the third hand …

But my nose still pointed and discerned.
When humans lay stuck to their blood
en masse, under birches, on cobbles
or vibrated with heat on bush timber,
I'd heard the cause yip in dance halls
and in national brigand lore: blurts,

then licensings, of underdog revenge.

Fusee

A complex iron finial-head
still dazzling from the forge
smokes in its ash and sparkles
in the shadowy workshop –
but no:

in fact it's a feathered
intricate protea bloom
haloed in a dusty ray of sun,
which in turn evades the stark
truth

that it's an incandescent
missile tamped in the choke
of an 18th century mortar, aimed
to ignite a timber city.

D.C.

City where aircraft are hung
as art, and security admits people
to the colonnaded floors
of horizontal beige skyscrapers
haunted by ideals and vast men.

Outside of the Iron Mask

Was any ruler ever a twin?
Even now you never hear of it,

a consort suckling one infant
in tears, after successive labours

and the bundling out of linen
– *O Madam, it is the State* –

nor her comfort: a far apprentice
ribbed for his likeness to a coin.

The Poisons of Right and Left

You are what you have got
and: to love, you have to hate.
Two ideas that have killed and maimed
holocausts and myriads.

The Top Alcohol Contender

An aircraft-engined kewpie doll
in chrome, with vast fat tyres,
stinks hotly of injection and rubdown
and little wheels splay at the far
end of its blood-red stick –
how else should it look,
the top alcohol contender?

Apsley Falls

Abounding white water
details each stratum
on basalt stratum
down hundreds and hundreds
like bands of washed linen,
this mummy standing up
the height of its mountain
in an ink-wet corridor.

To One Outside the Culture

Still ask me about adult stuff
when you want. But remember that day
in Madame Tussaud's basement
when all the grownups looked careful
and some young ones had to smirk?

You were right to cry out in horror
at the cut-off heads there
and the rusty dried trickles
shocked out of their eyes and ears.

Portrait of a Felspar-Coloured Cat

Plaintive, she named herself Min
in the reaching-down world.

Her texture manages itself;
her comet tail is Abyssinian.

All her intelligence
is elegance.

Never would soil she flicked up
persist in her belly fur.

Mars at Perigee

An apricot star
glittering, like a drop of desert rain
on the east night sky,
that was Mars at perigee;

the acrid sweet pulp around
the seed of a red passionfruit
was its taste on the mind

before any airtank thoughts.

More Pictographs

A beribboned question mark
is a *riddle*; one cut off sharp
and barbed is a *trick question*;

one bent over a magnifying glass
is *inspection*, or *investigation*
and one reversed is *answer*

but a tentacled octopus
with a human head
digesting life in its brain

is a mood. Which many have indulged
and there are hosts of words for
that mood, in the different lexicons.

Reflection in a Military Cap Badge

A pair of breasts in a window
as the Grenadiers marched by,
but were those breasts being displayed
by their own hands?

Explaining a Cheese

Explaining a cheese
she spoke in Australian English
but her hands spoke Italian.

National Dress

Ceremonial and truly ethnic
clothes may almost escape fashion.
For centuries on end
the hemlines of national costume
could allow women feet.

Before the Party or tourism
'national' meant local and peasant,
and in kingdom, tsardom
or *rzeczpospolita*, who needed
goose-satire on the train of a skirt?

Back before Hitler gave Poland
to his lawyer as a fee
for shameful relief
and got the fellow hanged,
who then wore national costume

daily and who once a year
mattered, in ways now lost.
Today, it's all identity,
all finery, with patterns a spring sun
might embroider in a park, and ribbons

in colours primary as principle,
but ancient mocking folk dance
sways in the light of forest
so deep it still breeds extinct
proto-cattle the shape of Lithuania.

A Shrine House

The past lives in a timber house
in off the road. A shrine house.

Tenants have never been let in there
and the car outside comes rarely now.

Paint from the first modern year
still strokes the shadowy best room

and in the silent talk of young parents
a slow broom isn't bunting cobwebs down.

At University

Puritans reckoned the cadavers
in Anatomy were drunks off the street;
idealists said they were benefactors
who had willed their bodies to science,

but the averted manila-coloured
people on the tables had pinned-back
graves excavated in them
around which they lay scattered in the end
as if exhumed from themselves.

The Young Fox

I drove up to a young fox
on the disused highway.
It didn't scare, but watched me
roll up to it along the asphalt.
I got out. Any poultry it would kill
wouldn't now be mine. No feud between us.

It watched quizzically, then bounded
away with an unmistakeable headshake
that says *Play with me!*
and stopped, waiting. I remember
how sharply perfumed the leaves were
that lay on the pavement in that world.

Experience

I heard a cat bark like a fox
because the car's larger purr
didn't soothe her, locked in a cat-box
and the hitchhiker said *We keep a snake*
to eat our rats! For heaven's sake.
I've heard a snake hiss like a man
I saw a goose sail like a bark
I heard a man wank like a goose.

The Barcaldine Suite

High on mountains worldwide they blow
on long wood trumpets in tones of psalm
summoning weirdness or cattle or calm
or play a wood horse with a horsehair bow
and the didgeridoo, that lowland shofar,
throttles where dancing and secrets are —

    Dance leaped from the Bang
    finding orbital speeds

    Life joined it underwater
    brought it skyward as reeds

    and half of dance air-dried
    into carolling and birds

    into drumming and howling
    and the human song, words —

Musicians mug outwards
dancing with their instruments
or stare deeply inward
communing with their instruments,
displaying the catch
or listening for the prey —

The band vamped along
to music pince-nez'ed to a tuba
and this woman stood in tears.
It was sunny Europe to her

and a Pentecost of tones
came to ignition over towns
getting nubs and gists uttered
that talk had often spattered –

Music is the great nonsense poem
written, for recital if at all,
in the old bonding lingo of cry
that we translate experience into
dilly-O Johnny Ringo bye bye
to check with the tree-nests of Home.

Music is the vast nonsense poem
our precisions float out on with emotion
to change and get poignant as they drown;
la Musique: it needs no translation.
It can back up, or send up, any Line;
it makes even the thought-police hum.

Tart angel that never lost Heaven
O waly the faraway wine
music is the great nonsense poem,

the religion no hard nose rejects,
not trapped in the medium of critics.
O harmonium the zillion-armed Om –

   Being deeply moved
   stops movement. Voice would be fur –

   The soul is open. Something
   always knew its key –

   laughter and crying at once,
   or rapt, or fainting to sleep –

   gooseflesh fades to shiver
   as the modern resumes –

I thought of ambient sounds that music has dipped up
in its silver ladle: heartbeats and hoofbeats, and trains
volleying with tipplers and Dopplers, or blue in the night,
drips in echoey spaces, wind through frightful places,
factory-crash heavy metal, the strung pluck of bows,
bells, whistles, the clinker coming at you across everything,
peaks peaks peaks of murder. And crowds, and the ocean snore.

It's a shortish list, even with the anvil and the cannon.
Has nobody scored the rippy un-tiling of a fish?
The colic in tennis courts? The blowfly race-call tune

that evokes no sex on a long flat saturday?
What about steamships, beyond the lorn siren to the barrel
and tumbledom of their nature, or the huge bulk gamelan
as hardwood logs collaborate into a keen sawmill?
Uneven steps rasping slowly, with rests, downhill?

   The weight of our weight
   the weight of our years –

I know the purist point isn't wild sound being redeemed
up into music, but what of music's own dimension
can be modulated into existence for the mind.
A body of its own for the mind, with no fixed visuals.
Without the beards and sweaters of hand-rolled wool
would work songs sound like politics? Would the symphonic,
without posh and penguin suits, still sound like a wall of money? –

   The weight of our weight
   the weight of our years
   the said and the shed and the
   stammered in tears
   and always this broadcast
   Otherworld at our ears –

Then, we'll be a tune
they'll put on and play
bits of and rarely

till our times pass away
and there's no one on earth
who knew us by heart.
Obsolete for all time
and that's just the start.

The Meaning of Existence

Everything except language
knows the meaning of existence.
Trees, planets, rivers, time
know nothing else. They express it
moment by moment as the universe.

Even this fool of a body
lives it in part, and would
have full dignity within it
but for the ignorant freedom
of my talking mind.

The Aboriginal Cricketer

Mid-19th century

Good-looking young man
in your Crimean shirt
with your willow shield
up, as if to face spears,

you're inside their men's Law,
one church they do obey;
they'll remember you were here.
Keep fending off their casts.

Don't come out of character.
Like you, they suspect
idiosyncrasy of witchcraft.
Above all, don't get out

too easily, and have to leave here
where all missiles are just leather
and come from one direction.
Keep it noble. Keep it light.

The Gymnast Valeria Vatkina

Legs counterposed like six o'clock, her stretch
is bowstave, sky foot to ground foot. A point shoe tips each.

She leans out around herself then, and gazes
intently past her hand at what she blazes:

a switchback trail of rainbow ribbon
that climbs stairs of air to her whipped baton

and equally shimmies down landings of allure
right-left right-left like a Caliph's signature.

The Aztec Revival

Human sacrifice has come back
on another city-island
and bloodied its high stepped towers.

Few now think the blood's redeemed
by red peppers, or turkey in chocolate.
Human sacrifice comes, now always,

in default of achievement,
from minds that couldn't invent
the land-galaxies of dot painting

or new breakthrough zeroes, or jazz.

Brief, That Place in the Year

Brief, that place in the year
when a blossoming pear tree
with its sweet laundered scent
reinhabits wooden roads
that arch and diverge up
into electronic snow city.

At the Widening of a War

Everyone was frightened of the sky.

Each night, Mars emerged at the zenith.
A bleb of pure rage tore off the Sun.

For days, the living and the dead
hung in the air like dust
whirled aloft from tired roads.

The fuselage of a lobster lay abandoned.

The Isles of the Blest were receding
to their sailing distances
and the gunfire of tourist shoes was stilled.

Sports stadiums and crowds loomed from another age.

The blow struck now
would be weaker than the blow withheld.

The Averted

The one whose eyes
do not meet yours
is alone at heart
and looks where the dead look
for a comrade in his cause.